HISPANIC STAR

SONIA SOTOMAYOR

CLAUDIA ROMO EDELMAN
AND **NATHALIE ALONSO**

ILLUSTRATED BY **ALEXANDRA BEGUEZ**

ROARING BROOK PRESS

NEW YORK

*For my mom,
who lost her battle to COVID,
but whose values live in me every day. I am
who I am because she was the best of role models.*

*For my husband, Richard, and children, Joshua and Tamara,
who surround me with their love, their belief in me,
and support. They make it all possible.*

*Most of all, this series is dedicated to the children
of tomorrow. We know that you have to see it to
be it. We hope these Latinx heroes teach you
to spread your wings and fly.*

—C. R. E.

*For you, young reader. May these pages inspire
your own bold, beautiful life story.*
—N. A.

Published by Roaring Brook Press
Roaring Brook Press is a division of Holtzbrinck Publishing Holdings Limited Partnership
120 Broadway, New York, NY 10271 • mackids.com

Copyright © 2023 by We Are All Human Foundation. All rights reserved.
Written by Claudia Romo Edelman and Nathalie Alonso.
Illustrated by Alexandra Beguez.

Our books may be purchased in bulk for promotional, educational, or business use. Please contact your local bookseller or the Macmillan Corporate and Premium Sales Department at (800) 221–7945 ext. 5442 or by email at MacmillanSpecialMarkets@macmillan.com.

Library of Congress Cataloging-in-Publication Data is available.

First edition, 2023
Book design by Julia Bianchi
Printed in the United States of America by Lakeside Book Company, Crawfordsville, Indiana

ISBN 978-1-250-82823-1 (paperback)
10 9 8 7 6 5 4 3 2 1

ISBN 978-1-250-82822-4 (hardcover)
10 9 8 7 6 5 4 3 2 1

CHAPTER ONE

DEEP ROOTS

"Everything about my culture has given me enormous education and joy."
—SONIA SOTOMAYOR

On June 4, 2010, fifty-five-year-old Sonia Sotomayor paid a visit to her childhood home. She had spent twelve years of her life in the Bronxdale Houses—a public housing complex in the Bronx borough of New York City that consists of nearly fifteen hundred apartments across twenty-eight buildings. Those project walls had seen her smiles and tears, her dreams and struggles.

This was no ordinary visit. Less than a year earlier, Sonia had broken barriers when she became the first United States Supreme Court justice of Hispanic descent. The Supreme Court is the highest court in the country, and to be appointed to it is a dream that many judges have—yet only a handful have achieved.

Traveling from the capital city of Washington, DC, where she worked, Sonia had returned to the Bronxdale Houses to make history again. The housing complex, which was home to many Hispanic families like her own, would soon have a new name: the Justice Sonia Sotomayor Houses and Community Center. For the first time, the New York City Housing Authority would rename one of its 335 properties in honor of a former resident who was still alive. This was a tremendous honor, and it showed how much the achievements of Sonia—a native New Yorker and the daughter of Puerto Rican migrants—meant, not only to the diverse Latinx residents of those houses but to the entire city of New York.

The renaming of the housing complex had been a true community effort. Residents of the Bronxdale Houses, housing activists, and local government officials had worked together to create a petition and gotten enough signatures to make the name change happen. Many of them—more than three hundred people in total—had now gathered for the renaming ceremony to welcome Sonia home. Shining bright in a red blazer, Sonia walked onto the stage to make her remarks as the people in the audience watched her with admiration, pride, and hope for what the future might hold for them, their children, and their grandchildren. These same walls also saw their smiles and tears, their own dreams and struggles. If Sonia could grow up in this housing project and later make history, what wonderful things might they and their descendants accomplish?

At the podium, Sonia fought back tears as she recalled "the hours and hours of laughter that my cousins and I had as we roamed the grounds of this housing project, and played in the playgrounds, and screamed and fought and laughed and lived."

She also highlighted the role that the Latinx community of the South Bronx had played in her life. "I am deeply humbled and touched that these houses will now bear my

name, and I am so grateful for all they have given me in my life," Sonia said. "The members of that community sustained each other and helped the next generation to grow. It is important for the broader community to remain committed to assisting the residents of this place so that other little Sonias will reach their dreams."

Sonia was certainly doing her part. During the ceremony, she danced alongside the youth choir from her alma mater Cardinal Spellman High School as its members belted out a gospel song called "Be Thankful." Later that day, Sonia also met with students at her former elementary school, Blessed Sacrament, and addressed the graduating class of Hostos Community College, where her proud Puerto Rican mother had studied nursing. Each stop on her itinerary was a reminder of how deep Sonia's Bronx roots ran and how much her community there meant to her.

Yet Sonia's story began unfolding many years before her birth, in a place more than sixteen hundred miles away.

Puerto Rico is an archipelago—a cluster of islands—that lies in the Caribbean Sea. It consists of a main island, four smaller islands, and hundreds of tiny landmasses called cays and islets. Puerto Rico is part of a larger group of islands known as the West Indies that also includes Cuba and the island of Hispaniola, which today is shared by two countries, the Dominican Republic and Haiti.

The Spanish words *Puerto Rico* translate to "rich port" in English. But the island's indigenous people, the Taíno, had their own name for their homeland in their Arawak language: Borikén. That is why, to this day, you will often hear Puerto Ricans refer to Puerto Rico as "Borinquen" or call themselves "Boricuas." The Taíno civilizations of Puerto Rico and the other Caribbean islands trace their roots to indigenous peoples who lived along the Orinoco River in South America (in what is now Venezuela), and long before the arrival of any Europeans such as Christopher Columbus, they had migrated by water to the islands of the Caribbean Sea over the course of thousands of years.

For centuries, the Taíno cultures of the Caribbean islands flourished. The Taíno of Borikén were skilled fishermen and farmers. They grew vegetables like yucca, beans, sweet potatoes, and other crops. The Taíno were also artists who made beautiful pottery and wood carvings and elaborate belts that they decorated with shells. A ball game played with a rubber ball was also part of the Taíno way of life. Today, Taíno culture continues to be an important part of Puerto Rican identity, and its influence is evident in English and Spanish words that have roots in the Arawak language.

EXAMPLES OF ENGLISH WORDS INSPIRED BY ARAWAK

ENGLISH	ARAWAK
barbecue	barbacoa
canoe	canoa
hammock	hamaca
hurricane	huracán
manatee	manatí

But the arrival of Christopher Columbus in the Americas in the late fifteenth century shattered the world of the Taíno. Working for the king of Spain, the colonizers enslaved the Taíno of Borikén and the other islands in the West Indies. Because the colonizers introduced diseases like smallpox, typhus, and measles into their communities, the number of Taíno people on the island dwindled. Today, there are vaccines that can protect us against these serious diseases, but for the Taíno, these illnesses proved deadly.

For three hundred years, Spain squeezed all the wealth it could from Puerto Rico—gold, as well as agricultural products like sugarcane, cotton, and coffee. The Spanish government showed no concern for the welfare of the island's natural resources or the people who lived there. In fact, the Spanish also captured and enslaved people from Africa and forced them to work in gold mines or on big farms called plantations.

In 1868, parts of the Puerto Rican population, including enslaved Africans, rebelled against Spain's oppression in what is known as the Grito de Lares (Cry of Lares). While the rebellion failed to achieve independence from the Spanish colonizers, over time Puerto Rico succeeded in gaining more freedoms, including the end of slavery in 1873—almost a decade after it was outlawed in the United States in 1865.

Though the first Africans had arrived in Puerto Rico against their will, they and their descendants have played important roles in the economic and political development of Puerto Rico and continue to add to the richness of its culture, from food to sports to the arts and everything in between. For example, popular dishes such as mofongo (made of mashed plantains and combined with chicken, steak, pork, or seafood) and bacalaitos (codfish fritters) hail from West and Central Africa, as does the musical tradition called bomba y plena.

NOTABLE AFRO PUERTO RICANS

JULIA CONSTANZA BURGOS GARCÍA
poet and journalist

ROBERTO CLEMENTE
Hall of Fame baseball player

ARTURO ALFONSO SCHOMBURG
historian and writer

SYLVIA DEL VILLARD
actress and dancer

Spanish control of Puerto Rico lasted until 1898. That year, the United States defeated Spain in a conflict known as the Spanish-American War. The war erupted after a US Navy ship called the USS *Maine* that was docked in Havana, Cuba, exploded and sank in February 1898. The USS *Maine* was stationed in the Cuban capital to protect American citizens in Cuba at a time when the Cuban people were revolting against Spain to gain their independence. Most of the crew onboard were killed.

At the time the cause of the explosion was not clear, but because the United States supported the Cuban revolt for independence, influential US newspapers immediately blamed the tragedy on Spain, paving the way for war. (Experts now believe the explosion was probably an accident.) After losing the war, Spain agreed to give up Puerto Rico and two of its other colonies—the Philippine Islands in Southeast Asia and the island of Guam, located in the western Pacific Ocean—to the United States in an agreement known as the Treaty of Paris of 1898. (Meanwhile, Cuba succeeded in gaining its independence from Spain.)

Since the Treaty of Paris, the relationship between the United States and Puerto Rico has remained confusing and complicated. In 1917 Puerto Rico became a US territory, and Congress passed a law called the Jones-Shafroth Act that recognized Puerto Ricans as US citizens. But the people of Puerto Rico have still been denied the right to vote in US national elections, and to this day they do not have voting representatives in Congress like American citizens who live in each of the fifty states do.

At one point, the United States also tried to "Americanize" Puerto Rico, in part by making children in Puerto Rican public schools take all their classes in English. But the people of Puerto Rico resisted this change and eventually kept Spanish as the language of learning in their schools, with English taught as a separate subject.

In 1952 Puerto Rico's status changed yet again. This time, it became a US commonwealth. This new status gave the local Puerto Rican government more control over running the island than it had had as a colony.

Under Spanish rule, poverty was everywhere in Puerto Rico, and it grew worse when the United States took over. At that time, many people in Puerto Rico survived by growing sugar, but under US rule, corporations took over the production of sugar from local landowners. Unable to make money off the land, a large number of Puerto Ricans needed to find jobs instead, but there were not enough of them. As a result, Puerto Rico fell into an even deeper economic depression, and many Puerto Ricans

THE US–PUERTO RICO RELATIONSHIP

The top elected official in Puerto Rico is the governor. In the early years after Puerto Rico came under US rule in 1898, this governor was appointed by the president of the United States. As a result, the first twenty-two governors of Puerto Rico were not native to the island and had no personal relationship to its people. In fact, the first Puerto Rican native to serve as governor of Puerto Rico was Jesús T. Piñero, who was appointed in 1946.

But Puerto Ricans demanded the right to elect their governor, just like Americans in the fifty states elect their own local, state, and federal representatives. And so, in 1947, US Congress passed a law allowing them to do so. The following year, Luis Muñoz Marín became the first Puerto Rican governor elected by the people of Puerto Rico.

Marín had once called for Puerto Rico to become an independent country. Instead, it was under his term as governor that Puerto Rico became a US commonwealth. As a commonwealth, Puerto Rico can pass some laws of its own. However, even though Puerto Ricans cannot vote in national elections and have no representation in Congress, the people of the island are still obligated to follow US federal law and pay some federal taxes.

were left with no choice but to look for employment opportunities elsewhere.

After they were recognized as US citizens in 1917, Puerto Ricans were free to move to the continental United States. As a result, in the 1940s and '50s, tens of thousands of Puerto Ricans left their homeland. The vast majority of them headed to New York City. A large number of these Puerto Rican migrants found homes in the northern part of the borough of Manhattan—so many, in fact, that the neighborhood soon became known as Spanish Harlem. Other Puerto Ricans settled across the Harlem River, in the Bronx, the city's northernmost borough. Though hundreds of miles away from their tropical island, these new Puerto Rican arrivals built a strong community and made New York their home.

Among the many Puerto Ricans who made the journey north in search of work during this time was a young man named Juan Luis Sotomayor. Juan Luis arrived in New York City by ship in 1944 during World War II, a global conflict being waged across Europe, Asia, and Africa. Juan Luis made the trip with his mother, Mercedes, stepfather, and brothers and sisters. He found a job at a mannequin factory. And, like other Puerto Rican migrants who came to New York City, Juan Luis and his family found housing in tenement apartments on Kelly Street in the South Bronx. He was happy with his job, but eventually that mannequin factory closed, so he took another job at a different factory that made radiators.

Juan Luis met Celina Báez at a party in the Bronx. Like him Celina was a young woman who had arrived in New York City from Puerto Rico in 1944 in search of new opportunities. Unlike Juan Luis, however, she came to the United States alone, leaving her family behind on the island. As World War II raged, the US Army recruited women to fill a variety of desk jobs that men left behind to go fight on the front lines. Celina joined the Women's Army Corps, and after she completed her training, the army sent her to New York City, where she worked in a post office, sorting mail and packages destined for American troops who were stationed in Europe.

Juan Luis and Celina fell in love. And she made it known that she was not planning on returning to Puerto Rico when her military service was over. So when Juan Luis asked her to stay in New York and be his wife, Celina accepted his proposal. The pair exchanged their vows at city hall in a small ceremony, and Celina moved into the apartment on Kelly Street with Juan Luis and his family.

Even after she was married, Celina wanted to continue

her education. During the first year of their marriage, Juan Luis worked at the factory to make money and support the couple while Celina studied to earn her high school degree. After that she studied to become a practical nurse—a nurse whose job is to provide basic care for hospital patients and help keep them comfortable. Then on June 25, 1954, Juan Luis and Celina Sotomayor became parents and welcomed their first child, a daughter they named Sonia Maria.

Sonia was an energetic child who started speaking and walking when she was just seven months old. She quickly developed a reputation for being mischievous, and her family gave her the nickname Ají, which means "hot pepper" in Spanish. By the time Sonia was born, her parents had moved into their own apartment in the same building where Juan Luis's family lived. The tenement where she grew up may have

been crowded, dark, and narrow with small rooms, but Sonia spent the early years of her life surrounded by her extended family, including Mercedes, her beloved abuelita. One of her cousins, Nelson, became her favorite playmate, and they spent hours together pretending to be knights, jousting in a medieval arena.

Spanish was the primary language spoken in the Sotomayor home, and most of Sonia's relatives spoke very little English. In fact, when Sonia was a kid, Spanish was everywhere. In the years since her parents had come to New York City, the Puerto Rican population in the Bronx had swelled. In 1953, the year before Sonia was born, migration from Puerto Rico reached its highest point with sixty-nine thousand Puerto Ricans leaving the island for the states.

When Sonia was three years old, her immediate family—which by then included Sonia's newborn brother, Juan Luis Sotomayor Jr., or "Junior"—moved to a new home. Their destination was a newly built public housing complex in the Soundview neighborhood of the Bronx that was owned and operated by New York City. It was called the Bronxdale Houses, and it was a ten-minute drive from Kelly Street, on the other side of the Bronx River. The move was Celina's idea; always striving to give her family the best, she was convinced that her children would have a better life in the new projects, which were brighter and cleaner than the old tenements.

Even after they moved away from Kelly Street, Sonia remained very close to Abuelita Mercedes, who loved to throw family parties on Saturday nights. Sonia looked forward to these parties. On Saturday mornings, Sonia usually went shopping with her grandmother on Southern Boulevard to buy all the ingredients—chicken, tomatoes, onions, and plátanos verdes (green plantains)—that Mercedes needed to whip up into a big Puerto Rican feast for her children and grandchildren. Arroz (rice), gandules (pigeon peas), and pernil (pork) were often on the menu. The dishes all started with sofrito, a potent sauce made with vegetables and an herb called recao. Years later, in her autobiography *My Beloved World*, Sonia would recall the whir of the blender as her grandmother and her aunts whipped up batches of sofrito in that Bronx kitchen.

On those Saturday evenings, while the adults played dominoes and listened to Puerto Rican music and her grandmother recited poetry deep into the night, Sonia played with Nelson and her other cousins. After the party, Sonia slept over at Abuelita's house. On Sunday morning, she would wake up to the aroma of homemade pancakes. "My Latina soul was nourished as I visited and played at my grandmother's house with my cousins and extended family," Sonia would later say in a speech. "They were my friends as I grew up."

As a child, Sonia was also very connected to her Puerto Rican roots. From the time Sonia was a toddler, she and Abuelita Mercedes would hop on a plane and visit the island. Sonia savored traditional Puerto Rican desserts like tembleque (a coconut gelatin) and fresh fruit like guava and mango during the day, then drifted off to sleep while listening to the soothing song of the coquí—the small frogs native to Puerto Rico that are considered a symbol of the island.

Eventually Sonia's mother, Celina, took Sonia and Junior on vacations to the island to visit her family. When they landed at the airport in the capital San Juan, the first thing they did was drink the quenching water of the fresh green coconuts that vendors sold along the roads. Sonia then had the vendor cut up the coconut so she could eat the creamy white flesh, too.

One of Sonia's favorite places on the island was the bakery run by her mother's brother Tío Mayo, who sold bread, pastries, and sweet, sticky guava jam. When not at her tío's bakery, she went to Luquillo Beach to dip her toes in the ocean. While she and her family often visited Orchard Beach in the Bronx—which was so popular with Puerto Ricans who had settled in New York that it became known as the "Puerto Rican Riviera"—Luquillo Beach was so different with its warm, clear waters, and fine, white sand.

In Puerto Rico, Sonia also loved to spend time looking at the works of art at the Museo de Arte de Ponce on the island's southern coast. For a young girl from an inner-city neighborhood, la Isla del Encanto (the Island of Enchantment), as Puerto Rico is known, was filled with wonders.

Sonia's childhood was full of love, but she wasn't always happy. Her father struggled with a mental illness called alcoholism. As a result, he drank more alcohol than is considered healthy. He rarely joined his family at Abuelita's Saturday evening parties on Kelly Street. And because of Juan Luis's drinking, Sonia's parents argued constantly. Celina spent many hours of the day away from their home and children, working nights and weekends as a practical nurse at Prospect Hospital.

Like many residents of the Bronxdale Houses, the Sotomayor family did not have much money. But Celina wanted to send her children to Catholic school, so she worked very hard to pay for their education. When the time came for Sonia to go to school, Celina enrolled her at the Blessed Sacrament Parish School, a short walk from the Bronxdale Houses.

At first, Sonia didn't like going to school and had little interest in her classes. She also felt strange speaking English at school, when at home she spoke only Spanish. It made her feel as if she didn't belong there. "It really takes

growing up to treasure the specialness of being different," Sonia would say years later. "Now I understand that I've gotten to enjoy things that others have not, whether it's the laughter, the poetry of my Spanish language—I love Spanish poetry, because my grandmother loved it—our food, our music."

Students at Blessed Sacrament were required to go to church for mass every Sunday. Most Sundays Sonia attend mass without her parents. When Sonia was seven, she stood up from her pew, like she always did when the time came to sing a hymn. But suddenly she found it hard to breathe, never mind sing. Everything—the priest at the front of the church, the booklet in her hand, the other parishioners singing around her—were fading, fading, fading until Sonia saw nothing but black. She had fainted in church! The nuns rushed over to attend to her and called her mother, who immediately took Sonia to see the family doctor.

After performing a series of blood tests, the doctor told Sonia she had a condition called type 1 diabetes. That meant that her pancreas, an organ that sits behind the stomach, was not working properly.

When we eat, our intestines break down food into a sugar called glucose and release it into the bloodstream.

A healthy pancreas makes a substance called insulin, which controls the amount of glucose in the blood the body needs. But Sonia's pancreas was not making as much insulin as it should. As a result, too much sugar entered Sonia's bloodstream, and that caused her to pass out during Sunday mass.

When she heard the news that her daughter had diabetes, Celina cried. At the time, when knowledge and treatment of the condition was much more limited, a diagnosis of diabetes was very scary, especially for a child Sonia's age. Celina worried that the illness would have a negative impact on—and even shorten—her daughter's life. Today, there are more and better treatments that allow people with diabetes to live fuller and easier lives, but when Sonia was diagnosed, she had to spend much time in the hospital to keep her blood sugar at normal levels. Every day, the nurses drew her blood with large needles and pricked her fingers to test her blood sugar. Sonia realized that she had a serious illness because her mother allowed her to miss school to receive these harsh treatments.

The good news for Sonia was that diabetes was treatable. To survive, she would have to receive insulin injections every day for the rest of her life. At first she needed only one shot each day, but eventually she would have to receive multiple injections every day. At times, Sonia's parents fought over who would give her the injection. Her father said he was afraid to hurt her with the needle.

One day the little girl, whose family had nicknamed Ají, became so frustrated with her parents arguing that she decided she would give herself the injection!

Sonia knew what to do because the doctors at the hospital had made her practice using an orange. The first step was to boil the syringe in a pot of water on the stove to make sure it was free of germs. Then she had to wait for it to cool down so she would not burn herself, fill the syringe with just the right amount of insulin—not too much, not too little—and make sure there were no air bubbles inside, because air bubbles can be dangerous if they get into our blood vessels and interfere with the flow of blood.

After patiently completing each step, Sonia bravely and successfully gave herself the insulin shot. From that day on, she gave herself a shot of insulin before leaving for school. At that young age, Sonia showed her parents that she could take her health into her own hands.

For a long time, however, she remained embarrassed by her condition and kept it a secret from her friends. Back then, and even now, people don't always talk openly about their health conditions because they are afraid to be seen as different and judged for their disabilities. But the day would come when grown-up Sonia would realize that having diabetes, or any other medical condition, was nothing to be ashamed about.

In fact, Sonia learned that sometimes the challenges we experience give us an opportunity to learn new things that we can turn into strengths. "Diabetes taught me discipline," Sonia later said during an event for the Juvenile Diabetes Research Foundation. And that discipline would enable her to achieve great success.

Learning how to give herself lifesaving injections was not the only hurdle Sonia faced as a child. When she was nine years old, Junior and Sonia came home from Blessed Sacrament to devastating news: Their father, Juan Luis, had suffered a heart attack and had passed away. He was only forty-two years old.

CHAPTER TWO

DESPAIR AND HOPE

"Experience has taught me that you cannot value dreams according to the odds of their coming true. Their real value is in stirring within us the will to aspire. That will, wherever it finally leads, does at least move you forward."

—SONIA SOTOMAYOR, *My Beloved World*

After Juan Luis died, Celina moved her family into a smaller apartment at the Bronxdale Houses. The weeks and months after her father's death were a very difficult time for young Sonia. Although the arguments at home had stopped, the yelling had been replaced by a heavy silence that was just as hard for her to bear.

Sonia and Junior saw little of their mother during this time. Grieving the loss of her husband, Celina came home from work to spend hours alone in her bedroom with the door shut and the lights turned off. Meanwhile, her children fell into the quiet cycle of doing their homework and watching television after school.

Becoming a widow with two small children at the young age of thirty-six was yet another difficult situation for Celina in what already had been a tough life. She had grown up poor in Puerto Rico. When she was a little girl, her own father had abandoned his family, and then her mother had died when Celina was Sonia's age. Now she was working six days per week as a nurse at Prospect Hospital in the Bronx to make enough money to support her family.

Sadness consumed Celina. When she was at home, she rarely spoke. In addition to her own grief over the death of her father, Sonia also felt frightened by the change in her mother's demeanor and resentful toward her coldness and distance. One night, Sonia couldn't take the gloom any longer. She pounded her fists on Celina's door. "Are you going to die, too? Then what happens to me and Junior?" she remembers asking her mother. "Stop it already, Mami, stop it." Then she sat on her bed and cried.

The next day, Celina surprised her children. When Sonia and Junior came home from school, she had turned on the radio and opened the window shades. Music and light filled their small apartment. Celina had put on makeup and perfume. Sonia's outburst had worked; her mother was making an effort to move forward with her life. Sonia felt better at home.

Sadly Sonia's beloved Abuelita Mercedes remained devastated by the death of her son. Unlike Celina, who eventually rose from her despair, Abuelita Mercedes was never the same person again. Although Sonia's grandmother moved to the projects, too, just a block away from where Sonia lived, she stopped throwing her Saturday night parties and reciting poetry. She wore black clothing all the time now. While they remained very close and Sonia visited her often, they no longer shopped together on Southern Boulevard. Instead, Sonia did homework and read books while her grandmother cooked.

In fact, books were becoming an important part of Sonia's life. The summer after her dad passed away, and while her mother locked herself away in her bedroom, Sonia lost interest in playing outside with the other kids in the neighborhood. She sought refuge in the pages of her favorite books.

"Reading became my rocket ship out of the second-floor apartment in the projects," Sonia said in a 2013 interview with National Public Radio (NPR). "I traveled the world through books. And even to this day, if I'm feeling down about anything, I pick up a book and I just read."

By now, Sonia had become a frequent visitor to her local public library, where she discovered chapter books. She especially loved reading comic books and Nancy Drew, a series of books about a teenage detective who used logic to solve mysteries. The adventures of this clever, puzzle-solving character who traveled the world made Sonia dream of becoming a detective herself. She imagined herself cruising the streets in Nancy Drew's blue sports car, searching for clues.

But comics and novels weren't the only types of books that captivated Sonia. In those days long before the internet made it possible to instantly look up information about any topic on a computer, people found information in big, thick books called encyclopedias. Just like a dictionary provides the meaning of words in alphabetical order, encyclopedias contain information about people, places, and things that begin with the same letter. Because of the number of books they contained, encyclopedia sets were expensive.

One day a man knocked on Sonia's door. He was selling volumes of *Encyclopedia Britannica* and convinced Celina to purchase a set. That Celina was willing to spend a chunk of her hard-earned money to buy the set for her children showed how much she valued learning. Years later, Sonia would recall vividly the excitement she felt when those encyclopedias arrived—twenty-four books in all. She devoured each one, becoming absorbed for hours in fascinating facts about science and geography. Her mind was a sponge, soaking up as much information as she could. "The world branched out before me in a thousand new directions," Sonia wrote in *My Beloved World*.

The fall after her father died, Sonia entered the fifth grade and found herself much more interested in school than she ever had been. Plus, she had a new motivation to do well in her classes. Her teacher, Mrs. Reilly, gave gold stars to students when they did something well. Sonia had a new goal: to collect as many gold stars as she could. She was so determined that she even asked a classmate to teach her how to study. Around this time Sonia began to wonder what kind of career she might have but also worried that her diabetes would limit her options.

Like any kid, Sonia enjoyed television. On Thursday nights, she watched a popular show called *Perry Mason*, which was about a lawyer who defended people who had been falsely accused of crimes. But the character on the show who fascinated Sonia the most was the young judge who ultimately made the big decisions in each case. "I realized that the most important person in that room was the judge," said Sonia in a 2013 interview with the *Today* show. "And I wanted to be that person."

WHAT DOES A JUDGE DO?

A JUDGE is a government official who runs a courtroom, overseeing proceedings and listening to evidence presented by both sides. That includes testimony from witnesses. The judge is an expert on the law and sometimes must issue a ruling—that is, make the decisions—as to what evidence and arguments can be presented in court, sometimes with the assistance of a jury. The judge is also responsible for making sure that the rules of the court are followed and that the process is fair to all sides according to the law. To become a judge in the United States, a person usually attends law school, passes a major test called the bar exam that takes two days to complete, and is appointed by an elected official or, in some states, elected by the people.

Sonia soon discovered that to become a lawyer and later a judge, she had to improve her public speaking skills. At a young age, she became aware that she had to "learn to speak persuasively and confidently in front of an audience." So when Blessed Sacrament began to look for volunteers to read from the Bible at Sunday mass, Sonia jumped at the opportunity. "It was a long way from arguing a case in a trial, but a small step in the right direction," Sonia wrote in *My Beloved World*. "And I had to start somewhere."

In 1968, the year she turned fourteen, Sonia graduated from Blessed Sacrament Parish School. At her graduation, she was acknowledged as the valedictorian—the top student in her class. Her motivation to earn gold stars had turned her into a model student.

Her mother wanted Sonia to continue attending a Catholic school, so she enrolled her daughter at Cardinal Spellman High School. During those first few months, Sonia had to take public transportation for an hour or more to get to school from the Bronxdale Houses, but her long commute was short-lived. In December of her first year of high school, Celina moved the family to Co-op City, a large housing development that was close to Cardinal Spellman. So close, in fact, that now Sonia could walk.

The new apartment at Co-op City was much bigger than their old place at the Bronxdale Houses. Their kitchen was large enough to fit a table for them to eat. A family friend helped divide one of the apartment's two bedrooms into two sections so that, for the first time, Sonia and Junior had rooms of their own. Still an avid reader and a fan of science fiction, Sonia chose a wallpaper covered with planets and constellations.

The summer between her first and second year of high school, Sonia continued to enjoy books but was itching to do more with her time off from school than just read. Even though she was legally too young to work, one of her aunts helped her get a job at a women's clothing store on Southern Boulevard called United Bargains. Sonia got paid one dollar an hour for putting clothes on racks and helping to keep the sales floor neat. Later she would work at a bakery across the street from Co-op City, filling the display cases with scrumptious bread and pastries.

At the same time, Sonia was more focused on her education than ever and was still looking for ways to become better at public speaking. By that point she understood that, as a lawyer or judge, she not only had to be comfortable speaking in front of people but she also had to explain her arguments and ideas to others with confidence. This required more than reading from a page like she had done at church during mass: Sonia also had to be convincing and hold the audience's attention.

With that goal in mind, Sonia joined her high school's Forensics Club. Members of the Forensics Club participated in different types of speech competitions, including debate. She was given a topic and then told whether she had to argue in favor or against a certain position. Her coach was an older student named Kenny Moy, who became a good friend and would play an important role in her life.

"Forensics Club was good training for a lawyer in ways that I barely understood at the time," Sonia wrote in *My*

Beloved World. "You got handed a topic, as well as the side you had to argue, pro or con. It didn't matter what you believed about the issue; what mattered was how well you argued."

As a member of the Forensics Club, Sonia also had to give speeches—without knowing in advance what the topic would be. Imagine how nerve-racking that must be! But Sonia learned to think on her feet. During one competition, Sonia delivered a speech about a group of people who had witnessed a crime and had done nothing to stop it from happening. When she finished, the audience erupted in applause. And after all the participants had delivered their speeches, Sonia won first place!

High school had a big impact on Sonia personally as well. Cardinal Spellman is where she met Kevin Noonan—her future husband. On their first date, they strolled around Manhattan. In Sonia's own words, they were soon "inseparable." Every day, Kevin would bring her a rose to school. (She later found out they were from her own uncle's rosebush!)

When Sonia introduced Kevin to her abuelita, that made the relationship official. Once Sonia brought him home to meet her family, it was understood that the couple would eventually get married.

One day, while Sonia was in high school, her mother announced that she was going back to school. She enrolled at Hostos Community College in the Bronx to become a registered nurse—a position that would come with many more responsibilities but would also pay her more money than her job as a practical nurse.

As a woman in her forties, Celina was much older than most of her classmates in the nursing program. But age didn't matter; she was determined. Celina's commitment to education would inspire Sonia throughout her life. "It's really hard with a mother like that not to think education's valuable," Sonia said many years later during an interview on *The Daily Show with Trevor Noah*.

Soon, Sonia had to think about her own education beyond high school. After he graduated from Cardinal Spellman, Sonia's close friend and Forensics Club coach, Kenny Moy, had enrolled at Princeton University in neighboring New Jersey. Kenny told Sonia that Princeton was part of a prestigious network of universities known as the Ivy League, and he encouraged her to apply to those schools, too.

> The IVY LEAGUE is a group of eight private universities located in the northeastern US. Except for Cornell University, which was established in 1865, all the schools in the league were founded before the US became a country. The group became known as the Ivy League in 1954, when they formed an athletic conference—meaning their sports teams play each other.
>
> - Brown University—Providence, Rhode Island
> - Columbia University—New York City, New York
> - Cornell University—Ithaca, New York
> - Dartmouth College—Hanover, New Hampshire
> - Harvard University—Cambridge, Massachusetts
> - Princeton University—Princeton, New Jersey
> - University of Pennsylvania—Philadelphia, Pennsylvania
> - Yale University—New Haven, Connecticut

Sonia knew she wanted to go to college outside of New York City. Although she had never heard of the Ivy League before, she took Kenny's advice. She hopped on the train and visited two Ivy League schools—Harvard University in Massachusetts and Yale University in Connecticut—but neither school felt right for her. Running low on money, she gathered up enough coins to take a bus to visit Kenny at Princeton. He showed her around campus, and Sonia fell in love with its vibrant green lawns, its castle-like Gothic buildings, and the surrounding wooded areas. Now this was a fit—the place Sonia wanted to spend the next four years of her life.

In 1972, at the age of eighteen, Sonia graduated from Cardinal Spellman High School. Once again, she was the valedictorian of her class. And not only did Princeton University accept Sonia in its class of 1976, the college also awarded her a full scholarship! That meant she would not have to pay tuition. Without the scholarship, Sonia would not have been able to afford to attend her dream school, which would have cost her more than $5,000 a year between tuition and housing. (For the 2022–23 school year, the cost of attendance at Princeton was over $65,000 between tuition and housing.)

Despite how hard she worked for these accomplishments, however, not everyone at Cardinal Spellman was excited for Sonia. The school nurse questioned why Princeton University had been quicker to offer admission to Sonia than to other students in her graduating class whose grades were just as strong as hers. Between her stellar grades and all the additional activities she participated in, Sonia knew that she had earned the right to go to Princeton because, while grades mattered, being involved in activities like the Forensics Club did, too. Yet the school nurse's hurtful suggestion that Sonia didn't really deserve to go to such a prestigious university would linger in her mind for a long time.

But many people in the community who knew Sonia were extremely proud of her. Those people included the staff at Prospect Hospital, where Celina worked, who collected money so that Sonia could treat herself to a little luxury: a new pair of shoes. And Celina celebrated her daughter's achievement by buying her a brand-new white coat as a gift.

Sonia was ready to start her journey at Princeton, determined to prove that she deserved to be there as much as anyone.

CHAPTER THREE

FINDING HER VOICE

"I am the perfect affirmative action baby. I am Puerto Rican, born and raised in the south Bronx. My test scores were not comparable to my colleagues at Princeton and Yale. Not so far off so that I wasn't able to succeed at those institutions."

—SONIA SOTOMAYOR

Princeton University is only a two-hour bus ride from New York City, but for Sonia, it was a world away. At that time, Princeton and other prestigious universities around the country were taking steps to increase the number of students who came from underrepresented communities. They sought to make their admissions process fairer for people like Sonia who showed the potential to do well at their universities yet may not have had the same advantages as their typical students.

This relatively new approach to college admissions was called affirmative action. The goal of affirmative action is to make up for the discrimination that has prevented some groups of people from achieving certain educational goals. Latinos are one of those groups, as are women.

Although affirmative action still exists today, from the beginning, some people have argued that it is unfair because it gives "special treatment" to people from certain racial and economic groups. That is, such people believe that the only reason these students are admitted to prestigious schools is because of their background and not because of their achievements. Looking back, Sonia recognized that the school nurse at Cardinal Spellman who had questioned her acceptance into Princeton probably felt this way about affirmative action and maybe even believed that Sonia took a place that rightfully belonged to someone else despite the fact she graduated at the top of her class.

Even though Princeton University had adopted affirmative action, there were few Hispanic students on campus when Sonia arrived in the fall of 1972. Most of her classmates were white, and many of them came from wealthy families. In fact, oftentimes the parents of these students had also been educated at elite schools—

perhaps themselves having gone to Princeton or another Ivy League university. When a student applies to the same college that a parent has attended, this is called a legacy, and the children of legacies have an advantage over other applicants whose parents went to school somewhere else or did not attend college at all. It is assumed that because their parents graduated from their college, their children will do well at their school, too.

Sonia was terrified at the thought of going to a school where she might be judged for coming from a low-income family and be seen as unworthy of being there. "When you come from a background like mine, where you're entering worlds that are so different than your own, you have to be afraid," she would later say in an interview on the *Today* show. But Sonia did not allow her fear to keep her from accepting Princeton's offer of admission or the full scholarship that made it possible for her to go.

Sonia soon discovered that many of her new classmates had experiences in their lives that had been beyond her reach. For example, they had grown up with money and could afford to travel all over the world, which itself can be a form of education. And despite Sonia's deep love of reading, they had read books that she had never heard of. Many of her peers had taken advanced courses during high school, and now that they were in college, they were signing up for higher-level courses than the introductory classes that Sonia was taking.

At first Sonia questioned if she deserved to attend Princeton after all, doubting that she was as smart as her classmates. Because of their previous educational experiences, they seemed to know much more than she did.

When Sonia got a C on an American history paper, and the professor who was teaching the course pointed out that she needed to improve her English grammar, she realized she had extra work to do. After completing her first year of college, Sonia spent her summer reading some of those classic books that her classmates had read in high school but she had missed out on.

Still, sometimes Sonia felt that she didn't belong at Princeton, no matter how hard she worked. Whenever she felt this way, she did what she had as a young girl coping with the loss of her father: She headed to the library and once again found comfort in books. But during the course of her first year at Princeton, Sonia had come to understand that she was no less intelligent or less dedicated than any other student there; the main difference between her and them was that she simply had not had access to the same opportunities in life as they had.

Being Latina and coming from a low-income family were not the only things that made Sonia different from many of the other students at Princeton University. She was one of only a few female students on campus. Princeton had not changed its rules to admit women until the fall of 1969—more than two hundred years after it first opened its doors! That meant that when Sonia walked through the gates in 1972, it had been only three years since the first women had enrolled at Princeton; they had not yet been there long enough to graduate.

A few weeks into her first semester at Princeton University, Sonia met another student, named Margarita Rosa, who was two years ahead of her. Like Sonia, Margarita came from a Puerto Rican family in New York City. The two women quickly became good friends, studying together in the library and bonding over pizza. Early in their friendship, Margarita tried to convince Sonia to join Acción Puertorriqueña—a student group Margarita belonged to that was committed to making sure that Puerto Rican students on campus could have their voices heard and their needs met.

To support each other, Acción Puertorriqueña worked closely with the Chicano Organization of Princeton, a group of Mexican American students, as well as other minority student groups on campus. One of Acción Puertorriqueña's primary goals was to recruit more Latinx high school students to apply to Princeton and support them during the application process. This was important work because most Latinx applicants to Princeton were not legacies; they did not have family members who had attended an Ivy League school and could offer advice and guidance.

Sonia didn't join Acción Puertorriqueña right away. Since she was new to college and felt at a disadvantage by the lack of opportunities she had during high school, she wanted to get settled first before taking on more responsibilities. Sonia's full scholarship also required her to get a job on campus. At first she worked in the cafeteria but later moved to the computer center. Back then, computers were new inventions, and few people owned them or knew how to use them. Sonia thought it was a "dream job" for a student, and she worked at the computer center during her four years at Princeton.

At one point during her first year of college, Sonia returned home to the Bronx to visit her mother. She found Celina anxious and worried about passing her final exams at Hostos Community College to complete her nursing degree. Sonia and her mother made a bet: If Celina passed her exams, Sonia would buy plane tickets for both of them to travel together to Puerto Rico.

Celina did pass her exams, and she and Sonia headed off to Puerto Rico for a two-week vacation. As usual, after getting off the plane, Sonia stopped to buy a fresh coconut from a roadside vendor. Now that she was visiting as an adult, Sonia came away more marveled by the natural beauty of Puerto Rico than she ever had as a child—not just the beaches but the majestic waterfalls of the island's rain forest, El Yunque.

Adult Sonia realized how invested Puerto Ricans were in their local elections and the political process. But she also noticed the extreme poverty that still existed in many parts of the island. During that trip, Sonia came to an important conclusion: Puerto Ricans in the United States and on the island needed to work together for a better future.

When Sonia started college, Abuelita Mercedes mailed her a dollar every week. During her second year, however, the envelopes suddenly stopped coming. Sonia soon learned that her grandmother had been diagnosed with cancer and was in the hospital. Sonia spent her Christmas break with her grandmother, and it would be their last time together. The death of her beloved abuelita broke Sonia's heart, and she returned to Princeton with a heavy sadness.

Now that she was in her second year, Sonia felt ready to join Acción Puertorriqueña, and by the spring of 1974, she had become one of the group's leaders. She wasted no time in finding ways to help the local Latinx community. Despite having a large Puerto Rican population in the surrounding town, the university had no Puerto Rican professors. Nor did it have any Puerto Rican employees working in its administration. In fact, there was not a single Hispanic person working for the university at all.

To Sonia and her fellow student leaders of Acción Puertorriqueña, this was unacceptable. The group accused Princeton University of discriminating against Hispanics in their hiring practices. The university's leaders ignored the group's complaint until Acción Puertorriqueña filed a complaint with the US Department of Health, Education, and Welfare. That move received national attention when the *New York Times* ran an article about the group's complaint. It quoted nineteen-year-old Sonia as saying, "Princeton is following a policy of benign neutrality and is not making substantive efforts to change."

Sonia didn't stop there. She penned another letter, this time to the university newspaper, the *Daily Princetonian*. "There is not one Puerto Rican or Chicano administrator or faculty member in the university," she wrote. "There are two million Puerto Ricans in the United States and two and a half million more on the island itself. Yet there were only 66 Puerto Rican applicants this year, and only 31 Puerto Rican students on campus." The pressure worked. Soon after, Princeton University hired its first Hispanic administrator.

Another issue Sonia raised in her letter was how little attention was devoted to Puerto Rico in the university's history courses. By then Sonia had fallen in love with the subject and had taken numerous courses. American history, European history, Soviet history, Chinese history—Sonia found it all fascinating. And yet at this prestigious and expensive university, she had little opportunity to learn about the history of Puerto Rico—her own history.

Sonia discovered that Princeton had once offered a course on Puerto Rico in the past. Eager for her and other Puerto Rican students to explore their history, she made it her mission to revive the class. It took quite a bit of work, but that didn't discourage Sonia. In order to get the history department's approval, she had to create a list of books for students in the course to read, find a professor who was willing to teach it, and get enough students to sign up for the class. But she was determined, and in the end, she succeeded.

In that class, Sonia learned more about how the people of Puerto Rico had suffered under Spanish rule and again, later, as a US territory and commonwealth. The class had passionate debates over whether Puerto Rico should remain a commonwealth, become a state, or seek its independence as other nations in the West Indies had—debates that continue to this day. It bothered Sonia that some of the books she read spoke only of the economic problems in Puerto Rico while paying little attention to the island's rich culture, which she had experienced herself on so many memorable family vacations. The books focused only on the people's problems and ignored their contributions.

As part of a class project, Sonia created an oral history of her family. That meant interviewing many of her relatives, and through these conversations, she collected stories she had never heard before about their lives in Puerto Rico and their experience starting anew in New York City. As a senior, Sonia wrote her thesis—a final paper required for graduation—on Luis Muñoz Marín, who in 1948 became the first governor elected by the people of Puerto Rico. She dedicated her senior thesis in part "to the people of my island—for the rich history that is mine."

Community service was also an important part of Sonia's time at Princeton University. She once read in a local newspaper that a Hispanic man had been sent to a psychiatric hospital in the nearby city of Trenton. He had been stranded at Newark airport in New Jersey when his flight had been diverted from its original destination. But because he spoke only Spanish, no one understood what had happened to him. In other words, the man had been hospitalized not because he was ill but because he did not speak English.

Sonia became angry at the way the man had been treated. She called the hospital and quickly found out that several other patients there spoke only Spanish. Meanwhile, the hospital had no Spanish-speaking staff to translate for them so they could receive the proper help. Recognizing that this was a difficult and unfair situation for those patients, Sonia knew she had to do something about it.

And she did. Sonia started a volunteer program in which students from Acción Puertorriqueña took turns visiting the hospital to serve as interpreters for the Spanish-speaking patients. This ensured that there would always be someone there to help them get the services they needed. Sonia and the other members of Acción Puertorriqueña also threw holiday parties for the patients, and she relished being able to improve lives. "The program in Trenton was my first real experience of direct community service, and I was surprised by how satisfying I found the work," she wrote in *My Beloved World*.

As a senior in college Sonia received a letter in the mail: an invitation to join an honor society called Phi Beta Kappa. At the time, she had never heard of Phi Beta Kappa and did not know that only students with exceptional grades received this invitation. Rather she thought the letter was a scam and tossed it in the garbage. Luckily a friend found the crumpled piece of paper in the wastebasket and explained to Sonia what Phi Beta Kappa was and what a rare honor it was to be invited to join. Recognition from this honor society was further proof that even if affirmative action gave her an opportunity to attend Princeton University, she was just as bright as any of her classmates.

That wasn't the only honor Sonia received while she was in college. She also earned the Moses Taylor Pyne Honor Prize, the highest award Princeton University gives to a graduating senior. As the winner, Sonia gave a speech at a luncheon for university alumni. Her mother, Celina, and her brother, Junior, made the trip to cheer her on. At that point Junior was enjoying success of his own while studying to become a doctor at New York University.

Also at the luncheon were Sonia's good friend Margarita Rosa and other Latinx students who had graduated from Princeton University in previous years. Still, when she looked up from the podium and into the audience, Sonia noticed how few Latinos were present. As she delivered her speech, Sonia hoped that at future luncheons there would be more Hispanics in attendance.

In 1976 Sonia graduated from Princeton *summa cum laude,* which in Latin means "with the highest distinction." This was another special honor given to the students who earned the highest grades in their class. Dreaming of becoming a lawyer and perhaps a judge, Sonia applied to law school. She ultimately chose to study law at Yale University—the Ivy League school in Connecticut she had visited as a senior in high school.

The summer after her graduation from Princeton, Sonia and her boyfriend, Kevin Noonan, got married at Saint Patrick's Cathedral in New York City. After the wedding, they moved into an apartment in New Haven, near Yale's campus. That fall she began law school at what is still considered one of the best schools in the country.

At Yale Sonia soon became involved with LANA, a student association for Latinx, Asian, and Native American students. Through a friend from Princeton, she also met

someone who would become an important figure in her life named José A. Cabranes. When Sonia met José, he was one of the most important Puerto Rican lawyers in the United States, having worked for the Puerto Rican government and then Yale University. José invited Sonia to work for him, and she helped him do research for a book called *Citizenship and the American Empire*, which is about the legal history of Puerto Ricans as US citizens and was published in 1979.

Meeting such an accomplished Puerto Rican lawyer inspired Sonia, and she would later describe José as her first real mentor. "A role model in the flesh provides more than an inspiration; his or her very existence is confirmation of possibilities one may have every reason to doubt, saying, 'Yes, someone like me can do this,'" Sonia wrote in *My Beloved World*.

At Yale, law school students were not given grades. Sonia set herself apart by contributing to the *Yale Law Journal*, a prestigious journal that published student work. Sonia proposed an idea for a paper that would explore whether, if Puerto Rico were to become a state, it would have a legal right to make money from the minerals and oils in the waters surrounding the island in the same way other states benefit from their own natural resources.

Having a paper accepted for publication by the *Yale Law Journal* is no easy feat. Being published takes considerable work and is a huge honor; many students try but few succeed. But the editor of the review found Sonia's topic promising, and she wrote draft after draft after draft until her editor approved of her paper. Soon after Sonia's paper was published, she became one of the journal's editors herself, which is yet another honor that makes a student stand out and increases the chance of their success upon graduation.

While Sonia experienced great success as a student at Yale Law School, she also got a taste of failure. After completing her second year of law school, she was hired for a summer position at a prestigious law firm in New York City. Being a summer associate is a big opportunity, and doing a good job can lead to a permanent position with the firm. Unfortunately Sonia found the work very difficult, and when the summer ended, the firm did not offer her a job. She was especially disappointed because many of her classmates had been able to turn their summer positions into permanent employment.

The failure caused Sonia again to question herself and her talent. "I had worked hard—I had and still do—but somehow that wasn't enough," Sonia wrote in *My Beloved World*. "And it was difficult to conclude that I was simply not in the same league as my classmates who were pulling in job offers from firms just like this one."

That summer had one bright spot. With the money Sonia earned as an associate, she and her husband, Kevin, were able to go on their honeymoon. They took a trip to the American West to visit friends, including Sonia's high school pal Kenny Moy, who by then was living in San Francisco. During their vacation, Kevin and Sonia explored parts of her country she had never seen.

And yet throughout the trip, Sonia could not stop thinking about what she considered to be a massive failure. With graduation from Yale Law School coming, she had to find work. While the shortcoming did not kill Sonia's dream of becoming a judge, disappointment over her first experience in a legal position made her very concerned over her next career step.

CHAPTER FOUR

FIGHTING FOR JUSTICE

"Few aspects of my work in the DA's Office were more rewarding than to see what I had learned in childhood among the Latinos of the Bronx prove to be as relevant to my success as Ivy League schooling was."

—SONIA SOTOMAYOR, *My Beloved World*

Unlike most positions, one cannot apply to be a judge. Judges are either elected by voters or appointed by a government official. To win elections and secure appointments, a lawyer must build an impressive career. Because Sonia had not succeeded as a summer associate in her first job at a law firm, she was off to a bad start. The failure showed her that she had a long way to go before she could qualify to become a lawyer, let alone a judge.

In 1978, during Sonia's third and final year of law school, a law firm in Washington, DC, hosted a dinner in

New Haven for Yale law students. Several Yale graduates worked at the firm, which had organized the dinner as an opportunity to meet and possibly hire more young lawyers upon their graduation. A friend of Sonia's who worked at the law firm suggested she attend the dinner, thinking it would be a good opportunity for Sonia to meet the lawyers who worked there and increase her chances of being offered a full-time job. The dinner turned out to be an unpleasant experience that once again forced Sonia to stand up against discrimination.

At the dinner table, one of the lawyers who worked at the firm asked Sonia how she felt about affirmative action. And like the nurse at Cardinal Spellman High School who questioned Sonia's admission to Princeton, he also asked her if she thought she would have been admitted to Yale if she hadn't been Puerto Rican, suggesting that Sonia received special treatment and did not deserve to be admitted to the school. It's easy to see why his questions angered Sonia, but she responded calmly, reminding everyone at the table that she had graduated *summa cum laude* from Princeton and was inducted into the Phi Beta Kappa honor society.

Sonia left the dinner feeling deeply offended, and while she had no intention of working for a company that had disrespected her, she proceeded with the next step in the firm's hiring process. The next day, she would have an official interview with one of their lawyers. Who was her interviewer? The same lawyer who had insulted Sonia at the dinner! While many people would hide their feelings in the hopes of making the interviewer like them, Sonia confronted him. "That was really insulting," she told him. "You presumed that I was unqualified before you had seen my résumé or taken the time to learn anything about me."

Sonia didn't stop there. Days later she went to the career office at Yale and filed an official complaint accusing the law firm of discrimination. When people on campus learned of her action, it caused quite a stir. Many of Sonia's friends and other Yale students supported her, but others thought she should have kept quiet. They were afraid that Sonia's complaint would destroy the university's relationship with the law firm and cut off graduates from potential job opportunities. Although Sonia never doubted that she had done the right thing, she did wonder if speaking up would hurt her chances of finding a job somewhere else.

In response to her complaint, the law firm formally apologized to Sonia in a letter. The *Washington Post* wrote an article about the incident, and once again, Sonia had stood her ground. She had shown that she would not tolerate discrimination, and by standing up for herself, she had also stood up for all Latinos. Her refusing to remain silent out of fear of losing a potential job may have spared future Hispanic applicants from that ugly experience she had.

Soon after that hurtful incident, Sonia had a far more positive experience at Yale. Eager for some free snacks, she wandered into a conference room on campus where she saw cheese and crackers being served. A well-known lawyer named Robert Morgenthau—the district attorney in Sonia's hometown of New York City—was giving a presentation to students.

A district attorney is a town's or city's top criminal lawyer whose job is to oversee the investigation that determines if a person who is accused of a crime should be held accountable for it. In a large city like New York, each of the five boroughs has its own district attorney who has many lawyers, called prosecutors, working for them to carry out these investigations. If a prosecutor believes they can prove a person is responsible for committing a crime, they will bring the accused to court.

From her experience as a summer associate in a New York City law firm, Sonia knew that recent law school graduates rarely got the chance to stand in a courtroom and argue a case before a judge. But Morgenthau told the Yale students that if they were hired to work for his office in New York City, they would be put to work immediately as prosecutors and be allowed to try cases. Longing to be in the courtroom ever since she was a kid at the Bronxdale Houses glued to *Perry Mason*, Sonia was excited at the possibility of working for Morgenthau.

Sonia chatted with him that evening, and Morgenthau was so impressed with her work at both Princeton and Yale, he offered her a job in his office. Her friends were shocked when she accepted the position. Unlike those who work at private law firms that pay very well, attorneys who work for the city earn little money. Despite the much lower pay, Sonia felt working for the district attorney was the right move for her, especially because it allowed her to return to her hometown.

Upon graduating from Yale Law School in 1979, Sonia and her husband, Kevin, moved back to New York. After getting hired by Morgenthau, one of the first things Sonia did was buy a red car. It wasn't a blue sports car like her favorite detective Nancy Drew, but owning it still gave Sonia great satisfaction. "I was the happiest camper when I saw that car," Sonia told NPR in 2013. "And when I got in it, I just imagined myself being Nancy Drew."

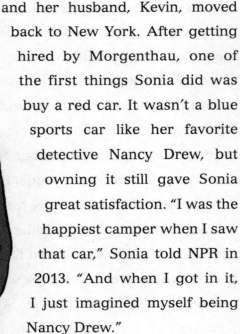

But unlike the fictional Nancy Drew, Sonia's work had real-world impact. In the US criminal legal system, an assistant district attorney determines how a person who has been accused of committing a crime is treated. They can decide, for example, whether to bring the accused to court, give them another way to make amends, or even connect them with services if they believe the person needs assistance rather than punishment to avoid breaking the law.

As an assistant district attorney, Sonia wanted to be fair but also compassionate in her pursuit of justice. She understood well that trials affected not only the victims but also the accused, their families, and the entire community. Sonia also recognized that sometimes people commit certain crimes because they struggle with poverty. That is, if they were not poor, they might not break the law. Therefore, meeting their needs was a more effective way of preventing those crimes than sending them to jail.

An important part of Sonia's job as a prosecutor was choosing jurors—the people who listen to the evidence presented in a trial and decide if someone is guilty or not guilty of the crime of which they've been accused. Sonia believed that some lawyers made a conscious choice not to pick Latinos or other people of color to serve as jurors because they assumed people from these backgrounds would be biased toward the defendant and vote not guilty. She was aware how such assumptions also suggested that Latinos and other people of color were not smart or thoughtful enough to serve on juries. So as an assistant district attorney, Sonia strived to fill her juries with people from all walks of life.

Less than a year into her job in the district attorney's office, Sonia's boss, Robert Morgenthau, suggested that she join the board of an organization called the Puerto Rican Legal Defense and Education Fund (PRLDEF). PRLDEF used the legal system to fight discrimination against Puerto Ricans. Sonia's mentor at Yale, the respected Puerto Rican lawyer José A. Cabranes, had helped create the group. This was volunteer work, meaning Sonia would not be paid for it. (Today PRLDEF is known as LatinoJustice but still has the same mission.)

Just like she had done as a member of Acción Puertorriqueña in college, Sonia saw PRLDEF as an opportunity to advocate for the Hispanic community in the United States—her community. Even though her work as an assistant district attorney took up much of her time, she became the youngest member of PRLDEF's board in 1980. In that role, she helped to oversee the work of the organization's lawyers who were going to court to win rights and fight discrimination against Puerto Ricans and other Latinos.

Sonia served on the board of PRLDEF from 1980 to 1992, and in those twelve years, it scored some significant legal victories on behalf of Latinos. Their first lawsuit required the New York City Department of Education to hire more Spanish-speaking teachers and offer bilingual education for students who did not speak English. This victory would benefit other communities whose first language was not English.

In 1981 PRLDEF filed another lawsuit that forced several of New York City's primary elections (in which voters who are registered with a political party choose nominees for offices) to be postponed. Voters who live in the same geographic area are organized into districts. The purpose of voting districts is to make sure every voter has an equal voice and gets the resources they need from the government. Over time, as people move around, the district lines must be redrawn to keep elections fair. PRLDEF argued that the way election districts were divided at the time meant that the votes of minority voters were not properly represented. For example, sometimes minority voters who lived in the same neighborhood were divided into separate election districts as a way to keep them from forming a majority. "Some of the victories won by PRLDEF—for voting rights, or against discriminatory hiring practices—would open doors for hundreds or thousands of individuals," Sonia wrote in *My Beloved World*.

Using her legal expertise this way was so gratifying for Sonia that she joined other organizations as well. One was the State of New York Mortgage Agency, which helped working-class families get mortgages so that they could buy homes of their own. Sonia also became part of the New York City Campaign Finance Board, an agency that is responsible for enforcing laws about how much money could be donated to candidates for public office, which is another way to ensure elections are fair.

As an assistant district attorney, Sonia worked long hours while her husband, Kevin, was studying biochemistry at Princeton University. The couple had moved to New Jersey, so Sonia took the train into Manhattan every day. Realizing they had grown apart, Sonia and Kevin agreed to get a divorce in 1983, although they remained good friends. Sonia eventually moved to Brooklyn, another of New York City's five boroughs.

In 1984 Sonia made another career change. As a prosecutor, Sonia had to work within the criminal legal system as it was. She eventually wondered if she could better serve the community in a position that focused on *changing* the system. "Maybe I should be working to improve it rather than simply enforcing it on the front lines," she thought.

With her eye still set on becoming a judge, Sonia also wanted experience practicing a different kind of law. So she quit the district attorney's office to work at a private law firm called Pavia & Harcourt. Rather than criminal law, she worked on cases involving business and corporate laws. Some of Sonia's work focused specifically on intellectual property law, which protects people's ideas and creations, from designs to inventions. For example, when a person or company creates a logo, it files a trademark with the federal government. This trademark is proof that they invented the logo and own it. That means no one else can use the logo without their permission or paying a fee to the owner for its use.

One day, practicing corporate law proved surprisingly exciting. During the 1986 World Series, Sonia had to hop on a motorcycle and chase a truck that was selling counterfeit Mets memorabilia outside of Shea Stadium in Queens, another New York City borough, across the river from the Bronx. Selling this merchandise was illegal because the vendors were using the team logo—the Mets' intellectual property—to make money without the team's permission.

Her experience at Pavia & Harcourt was a far cry from her first job as a summer associate. This time Sonia excelled at her work. In fact the firm made her a partner in 1988—which meant she now owned a part of the law firm and was entitled to some of its profits. Most lawyers who work in private firms strive to "make partner," so this accomplishment was another feather in Sonia's cap. But her best days remained ahead.

CHAPTER FIVE

A JUDGE AT LAST

"I will administer justice without respect to persons, and do equal right to the poor and to the rich."

—JUDICIAL OATH OF OFFICE

Although she was a successful lawyer, Sonia had never stopped dreaming of becoming a judge. While there are city courts and state courts, Sonia's goal was to land on a federal court where, as she'd learned in law school, the rulings could affect the entire country. "The federal bench was where matters of broad consequence, cases affecting far more lives than those of a victim and a defendant, were decided," she wrote in *My Beloved World*.

To become a federal judge, a lawyer must be nominated by none other than the president of the United States. It can take many years to be nominated, and even a stellar legal career is no guarantee of a nomination. Furthermore, there were very few Hispanic federal judges at that time. But for Sonia the chance to achieve her lifelong dream came much sooner than anyone might have expected.

One day, a partner at Pavia & Harcourt, a fellow lawyer named David Botwinik, told Sonia that the office of Senator Daniel Patrick Moynihan, one of two senators who represented New York State in Congress, was looking for qualified Hispanics to nominate for a federal judgeship. David thought Sonia should put her name up for consideration.

Sonia hesitated. She was only thirty-six years old—very young for a judge. She wondered if she was "reaching for far too much, too soon." For several months, Sonia did nothing. But her colleague insisted she apply, so she finally took his advice and filled out the long, detailed form describing her education and career up to that point.

Her effort paid off. Just two weeks later Senator Moynihan's office called Sonia for an interview with the senator in Washington, DC. She was one step closer! Many people, especially at Sonia's age, would have been intimidated by the situation, but not Sonia. A lawyer, Joseph Gale, who worked for Senator Moynihan and was present during Sonia's interview, later told NPR that she was "unflappable and completely poised, incredibly mature." He added, "Sotomayor knocked [Moynihan's] socks off."

Sonia impressed Senator Moynihan so much that he told her he wanted to recommend her to be a federal judge in New York. Sonia could barely believe it. "I floated out of the Russell State Office Building and wandered down the street in a daze," she wrote in *My Beloved World*.

After that, the president of the United States had to decide whether to nominate her for the position. On November 27, 1991, President George H. W. Bush nominated Sonia to the US District Court for the Southern District of New York. She was very close to achieving her dream, but there was still another hurdle she would have to clear.

OVERVIEW OF THE US FEDERAL COURTS

The FEDERAL COURTS OF THE UNITED STATES are divided into three levels. The first level consists of DISTRICT COURTS. At this level trials take place and judges listen to arguments and consider evidence such as witness testimony. District judges then issue a ruling on the cases they hear. However, lawyers who believe these rulings are incorrect can challenge them by filing appeals to second-level courts known as CIRCUIT COURTS. Circuit courts listen to these appeals and determine whether to uphold or overrule the district courts' rulings. The third and highest level is the US SUPREME COURT. Nine justices sit on the Supreme Court, and their decisions are final and impact the entire country.

As part of the system of checks and balances outlined in the US Constitution, which separates power among the legislative, executive, and judicial branches of government to prevent any one branch from gaining too much power, the US Senate must approve, or confirm, judges nominated to the federal courts. When the Senate confirmed Sonia in 1992, she reached her goal of becoming a federal judge! And her confirmation was historic in more ways than one. Sonia was now the first federal judge of Hispanic descent in New York State. She also became the first woman with Puerto Rican roots to become a judge on a federal court. And, at the time of her confirmation, she was also the youngest judge in that circuit.

Being a judge meant that Sonia made a lot less money than she did as a partner at Pavia & Harcourt, but that didn't matter to her. A judge is what she had always wanted to be. "I've never wanted to get adjusted to my income because I knew I wanted to go back to public service," Sonia said. "And in comparison to what my mother earns and how I was raised, it's not modest at all."

Now, like the judge in the TV show *Perry Mason*, Sonia was the most important person in the courtroom. But just because she had made it that far didn't mean that Sonia stopped facing discrimination. During her first few years as a judge, male lawyers often gave her advice that she had not asked for. Although Sonia was the most powerful person in the room, they did this because they doubted that a Latina woman had the capacity to run her own court. Other lawyers were outright rude and disrespectful.

"I had one lawyer who came to argue before me, and he was looking off to the side as he was talking," Sonia later told television personality Oprah Winfrey. "I started asking him questions, and all of a sudden he whipped around and looked at me intently. I could see in his eyes that he had finally figured out, 'This is no dummy, I'd better pay attention.' It is satisfying to see that."

Early in her career as a judge, Sonia had a health scare. She was celebrating her thirty-seventh birthday with friends in her New York City home when she suddenly felt light-headed and passed out on her bed. To those around her, she appeared to be asleep, but in reality, her blood sugar had dropped dangerously low. Sonia urgently needed to have some sugar to bring her levels back up, and luckily, she was able to grab some birthday cake in time. Almost no one at her party knew what was happening to her because Sonia had kept her diabetes a secret.

After that scary day, Sonia understood why the people in her life had to know that she was diabetic—for both her sake and theirs. "I realized that I should not hide my condition, not only because it was dangerous for me, but because if something had happened to me, and my friends were there, they would never be able to forgive themselves," Sonia said in her interview on *The Daily Show with Trevor Noah*. "It was a kindness to me and one to my friends, where I then chose to become open about my condition."

In her first few years as a judge, few of Sonia's cases drew national attention. Several of the cases she heard had to do with copyright laws, which she had specialized in as a law partner at Pavia & Harcourt. Similar to trademarks for designers and inventors, these cases fell under the category of intellectual property, which allows writers to claim ownership of their words, sell their work to others, and decide how that work can be used and by whom.

But in 1995, Sonia became famous nationwide because of her ruling in the case *Silverman v. Major League Baseball Player Relations Committee*. In August 1994 Major

League ballplayers went on strike, refusing to play games until they agreed on a contract with the league they felt was fair. The work stoppage lasted so long that the league canceled the 1994 World Series scheduled for that October.

In April 1995, with the start of a new season just a few weeks away, Major League Baseball and its striking players still had not come to an agreement. With no contract in place, the league intended to move forward with the new baseball season by hiring replacement players. The players claimed that the league's plan violated their rights as workers. Sonia, who had grown up rooting for her hometown Yankees and going to baseball games at Yankee Stadium in the Bronx, was randomly selected as the judge who would hear and decide the case.

In the end Sonia ruled against the league, stopping it from using replacement players. Her decision forced the league and players to continue negotiating until they finally agreed on a new contract. After that day, some people started to call Sonia the "judge who saved baseball." That may have been an exaggeration, but Sonia did play a key role in putting an end to the conflict so players could return to the field. That was great news for baseball fans everywhere.

Sonia had been a federal judge for six years when once again she was nominated for another judgeship. In 1997 President Bill Clinton nominated her to the US Court of Appeals for the Second Circuit, a court in the second level of the federal system. Although it took more than a year for the Senate to hold confirmation hearings and vote on Sonia's nomination, Sonia was finally confirmed to the US Court of Appeals for the Second Circuit in October 1998. Again she made history as the first Latina on that court. During this time, word started to spread that Sonia had a chance to one day be nominated to the most important court in the country—the Supreme Court.

Over the next ten years, Sonia heard *a lot* of cases—more than three thousand!—and wrote more than 380 opinions, which are essay-like documents that allow judges to explain how they made their decisions. In that time, she built a reputation for being a fair but tough judge. Known for asking many questions, lawyers who appeared in Judge Sotomayor's court knew they needed to come well prepared. Some lawyers found Sonia's style too harsh; she and others suspected this was because they weren't used to standing in front of a female judge.

As a judge, Sonia could no longer be involved with activist organizations like the Puerto Rican Defense and Legal Education Fund. That's because it would be a conflict of interest for a judge who issues rulings in court cases to also work with the lawyers who file lawsuits. Still she found other, small ways to give back to her community. As a gesture of gratitude, Sonia threw Christmas parties at the courthouse in Manhattan where she worked, with plenty of food and salsa music, like Abuelita Mercedes's Saturday gatherings. And everyone was invited—the security guards at the courthouse, the custodians who looked after the building, and the cafeteria workers who prepared meals.

Over the years, Sonia's work on the judge's bench continued to impress many people in government. When Supreme Court justice David Souter announced in April 2009 that he was retiring, her name emerged as one of the favored candidates to replace him.

"The minute I began to understand the importance of the Supreme Court, which really wasn't until law school, I also understood how unlikely it was to become a justice," Sonia told Oprah Winfrey. "It's said that you have to be struck by lightning. So it's not something you can live your life aspiring to. In the deep, deep recesses of your fantasies, you think, 'Wouldn't that be cool?' But really, it's just a fantasy."

Yet the fantasy was getting closer to becoming a reality for Sonia. President Barack Obama, who would be choosing Judge Souter's replacement, invited her to Washington, DC, to meet with him. After the meeting, Sonia returned to New York City and started packing, just in case. It's a good thing she did, because on May 26, 2009, President Obama announced that he was nominating Sonia Sotomayor of the Bronx to the Supreme Court.

When the president called her in New York to give her the news, "the tears started to come down," Sonia later told Oprah. "My heart was beating so hard that I actually thought he could hear my heart . . . I had my [right] hand on my heart, trying to quiet it. And it was the most electrifying moment of my life."

This was a big moment, not only in Sonia's life but also in American history. No person of Hispanic descent had ever been nominated to the Supreme Court. "When Sonia

Sotomayor ascends those marble steps to assume her seat on the highest court in the land," President Obama said when he introduced Sonia as his nominee, "America will have taken another important step toward realizing the ideal that is etched above its entrance: equal justice under the law." The president and Sonia appeared on the cover of the New York *Daily News* with a headline that referred to her as the "Pride of the Bronx."

Sonia's nomination created a lot of excitement in Puerto Rico, too. "I got a message from one of my friends in Puerto Rico, who said, 'Sonia, there's nobody working in Puerto Rico—they're all glued to the television,'" she later told *El Diario*, an important Hispanic newspaper in New York City.

CHAPTER SIX

THE HIGHEST COURT IN THE LAND

"I realized that people had an unreal image of me, that somehow I was a god on Mount Olympus. I decided that if I were going to make use of my role as a Supreme Court justice, it would be to inspire people to realize that first, I was just like them, and second, if I could do it, so could they."

—SONIA SOTOMAYOR, TIME

To become a Supreme Court justice, Sonia had to be confirmed by the United States Senate. During the confirmation hearings, she would have to answer tough questions about her past and her experiences as a judge. The confirmation process is important, because the responsibility of a Supreme Court justice is to determine if a law in question is in agreement with the US Constitution. Their personal beliefs should not play a role in their rulings. If enough senators doubted Sonia's ability to be impartial, they could vote against her confirmation and block her from joining the Supreme Court.

Sonia was ready to share her story with her country—and with the entire world. "I hope that as the Senate and American people learn more about me, they will see that I am an ordinary person who has been blessed with extraordinary opportunities and experiences," she said in the speech in which she accepted the nomination. "Today is one of those experiences."

In the weeks before the confirmation hearings, Sonia met with US senators, who would be voting on whether to confirm her nomination to the Supreme Court. She was on her way to catch a plane to Washington, DC, when she stumbled at LaGuardia Airport in New York City and broke her ankle. But after getting this far, Sonia refused to let an injury stop her. She showed up to her meetings with her foot in a cast and walking on crutches. But she was there.

For ten weeks in the summer of 2009, US senators debated Sonia's nomination to the Supreme Court. Based on common standards, there was no question that Sonia was qualified for the job. She was a graduate of two Ivy League universities, which many believe to be the best schools in the country, and had been an assistant district attorney, a private lawyer, and a judge for eleven years.

Yet despite all her accomplishments, the questions that haunted her throughout her life came up again. Was Sonia smart enough? Some people in the media and even in the Senate suggested the only reason she had been nominated was because she was Hispanic. Meanwhile, another candidate of a different background with equal or less experience than her might have never been doubted.

"At each stage there's been a sense, sometimes, that because you might have had a different life, that because you may have grown up poor, that defines you—and that you don't have the capacity or ability to achieve without a little extra help. That people have had to cut you a break so that you can be successful," Sonia would later say in her interview with Oprah.

Many of the questions Sonia faced during her confirmation hearings had to do with her time on the board of the Puerto Rican Legal Defense and Education Fund. Some senators suggested that her work with that organization was evidence that Sonia could not be impartial and would allow her status as a minority and her ties with the Latinx community to influence her decisions as a judge. In other words, they used her previous efforts to advocate for her own people as evidence against her appointment to the Supreme Court.

Although she understood that this was the way politics worked, Sonia wrote in *My Beloved World* how extremely hurtful these comments were. "To hear PRLDEF's activities so grossly distorted during the Senate hearings, with no regard for the good it had done the Hispanic community and the cause of civil rights generally, was painful to me, and to everyone else who had served on the board generously and honorably."

But in the end, when the votes were counted, Sonia prevailed. Of the ninety-nine senators who participated, sixty-eight voted to confirm her to the Supreme Court. From New York to Puerto Rico, people celebrated Sonia's achievement. For the first time since its inception more than two hundred years ago, Latinos finally had one of their own on the highest court in the land.

HOW ARE SUPREME COURT JUSTICES CHOSEN?

Supreme Court justices are nominated by the president of the United States and confirmed by the US Senate. Judges who are appointed to the Supreme Court serve for life or until they retire. This is important, because it means that judges can make their decisions without fear that they may lose their jobs. As a result, Supreme Court justices usually remain in their roles for years, even decades, after the president and senators who nominated and confirmed them have left office. The rulings

> they make impact the lives of Americans long after they retire or die. Because of this tremendous power, the nomination and confirmation of Supreme Court justices always spark great debates, as everyone wants the candidate to be someone who they believe shares their views.

On August 8, 2009, with her mother, Celina; her brother, Junior; her sister-in-law, Tracey; and her niece and two nephews in attendance, Sonia was sworn in as the 111th Supreme Court justice in US history, and the first of Hispanic descent. At the time, Sonia was also only the third woman to be named to the Supreme Court, following Sandra Day O'Connor and Ruth Bader Ginsburg. Other women would later follow.

At a private ceremony in Washington, DC, Celina held a copy of the Bible as Sonia placed her hand on it and swore to uphold the US Constitution. She would get to work soon, but first it was time for her to celebrate. Back in New York City, celebrities threw a dinner party in Sonia's honor. She appeared on magazine covers and was invited to throw out the first pitch at Yankee Stadium. Everyone, especially Latinos, was talking about Sonia.

The girl from the Bronx had attained the highest position a judge in the United States could aspire to. That didn't mean she wasn't afraid. But just like she had done as a student at Princeton and Yale, and throughout her career as a lawyer and a judge, Sonia did not let fear stop her. In fact she did what she had always done to overcome her fears.

She immediately started asking questions.

SCHUETTE V. COALITION TO DEFEND AFFIRMATIVE ACTION

During her time on the Supreme Court, Sonia has often made headlines for her passionate arguments even when she has disagreed with the majority ruling. In 2014, for example, in the case *Schuette v. Coalition to Defend Affirmative Action*, the Supreme Court ruled in a 6–2 decision that it was constitutional for states to pass laws that banned affirmative action at colleges and universities—the same kind of programs that enabled Sonia to attend Princeton University all those years ago.

As one of two dissenting justices—the other was Ruth Bader Ginsburg—Sonia disagreed with the majority's decision. In a long, passionate dissent that ran for fifty-eight pages, she argued that limits on affirmative action hurt Latinos and other racial minorities when they applied to colleges and universities. She believed that the Supreme Court was ignoring the racial discrimination that these groups face when trying to access higher education.

"This refusal to accept the stark reality that race matters is regrettable," Sonia wrote in her dissent. "The way to stop discrimination on the basis of race is to speak openly and candidly on the subject of race, and to apply the Constitution with eyes open to the unfortunate effects of centuries of racial discrimination." In other words, Sonia disagreed with the opinion that the way to eliminate racism was to act as if events of the past no longer had negative effects in the present day. Instead she believed that the way to end discrimination was to accept that it still takes place and use our laws to address this problem.

Breaking ground comes with great responsibility. From the moment she took the oath as the first Supreme Court justice of Hispanic descent in US history, Sonia became a role model, not just for Puerto Ricans but also Latinos in general. "She carries the hopes of more than fifty million people,"

a lawyer and close friend of Sonia's, Carlos Ortiz, said in 2009, referring to the number of Latinos living in the United States at the time. As of 2020, the number has grown to 62.1 million.

Sonia has not only accepted that responsibility—she has embraced it. Trailblazers don't always want to be role models, but Sonia is committed to speaking honestly about her struggles in life. She has especially made it a point to inspire and uplift children—"little Sonias," as she said in her speech at the Bronxdale House renaming ceremony—to accomplish their own dreams and make a difference in the world.

One way she has done this is through books. Sonia's love of reading inspired her to write multiple books for children. Her first children's book, called *Turning Pages: My Life Story*, describes the important role that books have played in her life. She also wrote the books *Just Ask!* and *Just Help!*, which encourage readers to reach out to others who might be excluded and to take action, however small, to improve their communities. Sonia also has appeared on the children's television show *Sesame Street* so kids can see how far someone like her can go.

In her interview on *The Daily Show with Trevor Noah*, Sonia explained why reaching out to young people is so important to her: "If I can affect the lives of children, if I can inspire them to be bigger, better, braver than they believe they can be, then I've left a real legacy."

DID YOU KNOW?

★ Not only is Justice Sotomayor the first Hispanic US Supreme Court justice, but she is also the third female justice in US Supreme Court history after Justices Sandra Day O'Connor (nominated in 1981) and Ruth Bader Ginsburg (nominated in 1993).

edition.cnn.com/2013/03/08/us/sonia-sotomayor-fast-facts/index.html

★ On January 20, 2021, Sotomayor swore in Kamala Harris, the first female, first Black, and first South Asian US vice president.

edition.cnn.com/2013/03/08/us/sonia-sotomayor-fast-facts/index.html

★ During 2012, while already on the Supreme Court, Sotomayor made two appearances as herself on the children's television program *Sesame Street*, explaining what a vocational career is and then demonstrating how a judge hears a case.

youtube.com/watch?v=EHICz5MYxNQ

youtube.com/watch?v=FizspmIJbAw

★ Justice Sotomayor has written five books: her 2013 memoir, *My Beloved World*, and four books for children: *The Beloved World of Sonia Sotomayor*; *Turning Pages: My Life Story*; *Just Ask! Be Different, Be Brave, Be You*; and *Just Help! How to Build a Better World*. All five were published in both English and Spanish.

oprahdaily.com/entertainment/a35256242

/justice-sonia-sotomayor-facts/

★ In 2013, a painting featuring Sonia, Sandra Day O'Connor, Ruth Bader Ginsburg, and Elena Kagan was unveiled at the Smithsonian's National Portrait Gallery in Washington, DC. Titled "The Four Justices," the painting is a tribute to the first four female justices who have served on the US Supreme Court. The painting measures approximately seven feet by five-and-a-half feet, but with its custom-made frame, it's even larger at almost nine-and-a-half feet by eight feet.

npg.si.edu/exhibit/fourjustices/

★ On New Year's Eve in 2013, Justice Sotomayor led the countdown and pushed the button that drops the famed crystal ball in New York City's Times Square, ringing in 2014.

> foxnews.com/world/supreme-court-justice-sonia-sotomayor
> -drops-ball-and-gavel-on-new-years-eve

★ Sonia Sotomayor loves salsa dancing. She famously got Chief Justice John Roberts to dance with her for an end-of-term celebration, breaking tradition.

> usnews.com/news/blogs/washington-whispers/2014
> /10/08/sonia-sotomayor-brings-salsa-trouble-to
> -the-supreme-court

★ In 2019, Sotomayor was inducted into the National Women's Hall of Fame.

> womenofthehall.org/women-of-the-hall/?keyword
> =sotomayor&view=photos

A NOTE FROM CLAUDIA ROMO EDELMAN

Affirmative action is a set of procedures designed to eliminate unlawful discrimination. Its goal is to remedy the results of such prior discrimination and also prevent it in the future. Sonia Sotomayor was the beneficiary of an affirmative action program for admission to an educational program, but such programs can also exist for professional development and even legislative seats or political positions.

At the end of October 2022, the Supreme Court heard both arguments for and against the constitutionality of affirmative action in higher education. This means that the court will interpret the laws and decide if affirmative action upholds the fundamental values of the nation as embedded in the Constitution and the Bill of Rights.

This is not the first time affirmative action has reached the Supreme Court; it is a topic that has been discussed since 1954. We encourage our young readers to learn more about this subject and its history in our country and to keep track of the case as it makes the news. Most importantly, I encourage you to reflect on the effect of affirmative action on your family, your school, and your community. Ask yourself, what is the meaning of equality and who has had access to it in our country? Who would have less or more of an opportunity without affirmative action? What is the meaning of equal opportunity?

A NOTE FROM NATHALIE ALONSO

In 2019, when my journey as a children's book author was just beginning, I attended a Society of Children's Book Writers and Illustrators (SCBWI) conference in New York City. Among the speakers that weekend was none other than Supreme Court Justice Sonia Sotomayor, whose achievements include publishing multiple books for young people. As I listened to her discuss the role that literature had played in her life and her decision to turn her personal stories into children's books, it dawned on me that if I ever became a published children's author, there would be yet another parallel between my life and hers.

You see, like Sonia, I was born in a New York City outer borough (Queens). Like Sonia, my family comes from a Caribbean island (Cuba). Like Sonia, I was a book-loving kid who grew up speaking Spanish at home. Like Sonia, I went to an Ivy League school (Columbia University) on a scholarship. As someone who grew up without representation, it's hard to overstate how meaningful and validating Sonia's Supreme Court appointment was for me.

However, I could not have imagined that soon after that SCBWI conference, I would be writing a book about Sonia. As I learned more about her experiences as a Latina making inroads in spaces that had not been built for women of color, I developed a deeper understanding of the forces that have shaped my own life and a greater appreciation of my own place in the world—an incredible gift. So it is with immense honor and gratitude that I contribute this title to the Hispanic Star series.

A NOTE FROM HISPANIC STAR

When Hispanic Star decided to join Macmillan and Roaring Brook Press in creating this chapter book biography series, our intention was to share stories of incredible Hispanic leaders with young readers, inspiring them through the acts of those Stars. For centuries, the Hispanic community has made significant contributions to different spaces of our collective culture—whether it's sports, entertainment, art, politics, or business—and we wanted to showcase some of the role models who made this possible. We especially wanted to inspire Latinx children to rise up and take the mantle of Hispanic unity and pride.

With Hispanic Star, we also wanted to shine a light on the common language that unifies a large portion of the Latinx community. *Hispanic* means "Spanish speaking" and frequently refers to people whose origins are from a country where Spanish is the primary spoken language. The term *Latinx*, in all its ever-changing deviations, refers to people of all gender identities from all countries in Latin America and their descendants, many of them already born in the United States.

This groundbreaking book series can be found both in English and Spanish as a tribute to the Hispanic community in our country.

We encourage all of our readers to get to know these heroes and the positive impact they continue to have, inviting future generations to learn more about the different journeys of our unique and charming Hispanic Stars!

THE HISPANIC STAR SERIES

Read about the most groundbreaking, iconic Hispanic heroes who have shaped our culture and the world in this gripping biography series for young readers.

IF YOU CAN SEE IT, YOU CAN BE IT.